Francis Browm, Roswell Dwight Hitchcocck

Teaching of the Twelve Apostles

Francis Browm, Roswell Dwight Hitchcocck

Teaching of the Twelve Apostles

ISBN/EAN: 9783744685276

Printed in Europe, USA, Canada, Australia, Japan

Cover: Foto ©Lupo / pixelio.de

More available books at **www.hansebooks.com**

ΔΙΔΑΧΗ
ΤΩΝ ΔΩΔΕΚΑ ΑΠΟΣΤΟΛΩΝ.

TEACHING

OF

THE TWELVE APOSTLES.

*RECENTLY DISCOVERED AND PUBLISHED BY PHILOTHEOS
BRYENNIOS, METROPOLITAN OF NICOMEDIA.*

EDITED WITH A TRANSLATION, INTRODUCTION
AND NOTES,

BY

ROSWELL D. HITCHCOCK

AND

FRANCIS BROWN,

PROFESSORS IN UNION THEOLOGICAL SEMINARY, NEW YORK.

NEW YORK:
CHARLES SCRIBNER'S SONS.
1884.

INTRODUCTION.

In 1875 Philotheos Bryennios, then Metropolitan of Serrae (now Serres), in ancient Macedonia, published the two Epistles of Clement of Rome, from a manuscript discovered by him in the Library of the Most Holy Sepulchre in Fanar of Constantinople. The last six chapters (60–65) of the First Epistle, and the last eight sections (13–20) of the so-called Second Epistle, had never been published before. The date of the manuscript is 1056 A.D. As described by the finder, "it is an octavo volume, written on

parchment, in cursive characters, and consists of 120 leaves." First comes Chrysostom's Synopsis of the Books of the Old and New Testament; then the Epistle of Barnabas; then the two Epistles of Clement; then the Teaching of the Twelve Apostles; then the Epistle of Mary of Cassobelae to Ignatius; followed by twelve Epistles of Ignatius (the current seven, besides one to the Virgin Mary, and four others).

The "Teaching of the Twelve Apostles," Διδαχὴ τῶν δώδεκα Ἀποστόλων, occupies leaves 76–80 of the manuscript. It now seems strange to us that the document thus announced attracted so little attention. This same Bryennios, now Metropolitan of Nicomedia, in Asia Minor, has again surprised the literary world by publishing, with an abundance of learned illustration, this long-lost document. It is printed in Constantinople, and the date of publication is 1883. The genuineness of the document can hardly be doubted. It is cited by Clement of Alexandria in his First Stroma; by Eusebius,

who speaks of it (Hist. iii. 25) as τῶν Ἀποστόλων αἱ λεγόμεναι διδαχαί; and by Athanasius
in his 39th Festal Epistle. Bickell and Geb-
hardt had recently argued that there must have
been some such document underlying both the
Seventh Book of the Apostolic Constitutions
and the Apostolic Epitome. In 1882 Kra-
wutzky undertook, from these sources, to re-
cover and reconstruct the embedded earlier and
simpler document; and with a success of the
most pronounced and brilliant character, as now
tested by the work just published.

This document belongs undoubtedly to the
second century; possibly as far back as 120
A.D., hardly later than 160 A.D. The whole tone
of it is archaic. It contradicts nothing belong-
ing to that age; corroborates some things which
may henceforth be more strongly emphasized;
and adds some things for which we may well
be very profoundly grateful.

The present editors are happy to be able to
put this "Teaching of the Twelve Apostles" so

promptly before the American public. The text has been carefully edited. The translation will be found to be studiously literal. A few notes have been added, which, it is hoped, may be of service both to students and to general readers.

ROSWELL D. HITCHCOCK.

FRANCIS BROWN.

UNION THEOLOGICAL SEMINARY,
NEW YORK CITY, March 20, 1884.

ΔΙΔΑΧΗ

ΤΩΝ ΔΩΔΕΚΑ ΑΠΟΣΤΟΛΩΝ.

ΔΙΔΑΧΗ

ΤΩΝ

ΔΩΔΕΚΑ ΑΠΟΣΤΟΛΩΝ.

Διδαχὴ Κυρίου διὰ τῶν δώδεκα ἀποστόλων τοῖς ἔθνεσιν.

Κεφ. α΄. Ὁδοὶ δύο εἰσί, μία τῆς ζωῆς καὶ μία τοῦ θανά-
τον, διαφορὰ δὲ πολλὴ μεταξὺ τῶν δύο ὁδῶν.
5 Ἡ μὲν οὖν ὁδὸς τῆς ζωῆς ἐστιν αὕτη· πρῶτον,
ἀγαπήσεις τὸν Θεὸν τὸν ποιήσαντά σε· δεύτε-
ρον, τὸν πλησίον σου ὡς σεαυτόν· πάντα δὲ ὅσα
ἐὰν θελήσῃς μὴ γίνεσθαί σοι, καὶ σὺ ἄλλῳ μὴ
ποίει. Τούτων δὲ τῶν λόγων ἡ διδαχή ἐστιν
10 αὕτη· Εὐλογεῖτε τοὺς καταρωμένους ὑμῖν καὶ
προσεύχεσθε ὑπὲρ τῶν ἐχθρῶν ὑμῶν, νηστεύετε
δὲ ὑπὲρ τῶν διωκόντων ὑμᾶς· ποία γὰρ χάρις,

TEACHING

OF THE

TWELVE APOSTLES.

— · ——————

TEACHING OF THE LORD, THROUGH THE TWELVE APOS-
TLES, TO THE NATIONS.

CHAP. I.—Two ways there are, one of life and one of
death, but there is a great difference between the two
ways. The way of life, then, is this: First, thou shalt
love the God who made thee; secondly, thy neighbor
as thyself; and all things whatsoever thou wouldst not
have befall thee, thou, too, do not to another. Now
of these words the teaching is this: Bless them that
curse you, and pray for your enemies, and fast for
them that persecute you: for what thank *have ye* if ye

3

ἐὰν ἀγαπᾶτε τοὺς ἀγαπῶντας ὑμᾶς; οὐχὶ καὶ τὰ
ἔθνη τὸ αὐτὸ ποιοῦσιν; ὑμεῖς δὲ ἀγαπᾶτε τοὺς
15 μισοῦντας ὑμᾶς καὶ οὐχ ἕξετε ἐχθρόν. Ἀπέχου
τῶν σαρκικῶν καὶ κοσμικῶν ἐπιθυμιῶν. Ἐάν
τις σοι δῷ ῥάπισμα εἰς τὴν δεξιὰν σιαγόνα,
στρέψον αὐτῷ καὶ τὴν ἄλλην, καὶ ἔσῃ τέλειος·
ἐὰν ἀγγαρεύσῃ σέ τις μίλιον ἕν, ὕπαγε μετ᾽ αὐ-
20 τοῦ δύο· ἐὰν ἄρῃ τις τὸ ἱμάτιόν σου, δὸς αὐτῷ
καὶ τὸν χιτῶνα· ἐὰν λάβῃ τις ἀπὸ σοῦ τὸ σόν,
μὴ ἀπαίτει· οὐδὲ γὰρ δύνασαι. Παντὶ τῷ αἰ-
τοῦντί σε δίδου καὶ μὴ ἀπαίτει· πᾶσι γὰρ θέλει
δίδοσθαι ὁ πατὴρ ἐκ τῶν ἰδίων χαρισμάτων.
25 Μακάριος ὁ διδοὺς κατὰ τὴν ἐντολήν· ἀθῷος
γάρ ἐστιν· οὐαὶ τῷ λαμβάνοντι· εἰ μὲν γὰρ
χρείαν ἔχων λαμβάνει τις, ἀθῷος ἔσται· ὁ δὲ
μὴ χρείαν ἔχων δώσει δίκην, ἱνατί ἔλαβε καὶ εἰς
τί, ἐν συνοχῇ δὲ γενόμενος ἐξετασθήσεται περὶ
30 ὧν ἔπραξε, καὶ οὐκ ἐξελεύσεται ἐκεῖθεν μέχρις
οὗ ἀποδῷ τὸν ἔσχατον κοδράντην. Ἀλλὰ καὶ
περὶ τούτου δὴ εἴρηται· Ἱδρωσάτω ἡ ἐλεημοσύ-
νη σου εἰς τὰς χεῖράς σου, μέχρις ἂν γνῷς τίνι
δῷς.

35 Κεφ. β΄. Δευτέρα δὲ ἐντολὴ τῆς διδαχῆς Οὐ φονεύσεις,
οὐ μοιχεύσεις, οὐ παιδοφθορήσεις, οὐ πορνεύσεις,

4

love them that love you? Do not the nations also the same? But love ye them that hate you and ye shall have no enemy. Abstain from the fleshly and worldly lusts. If any one give thee a blow on the right cheek, turn to him the other also, and thou shalt be perfect; if any one compel thee to go one mile, go with him two; if any one take thy cloak, give him thy tunic also; if any one take from thee what is thine, ask it not back; for indeed thou canst not. To every one that asketh thee give, and ask not back; for to all the Father desires to give of his own gracious gifts. Blessed is he that giveth according to the commandment; for he is guiltless; wo to him that taketh; for if, indeed, one taketh who hath need, he shall be guiltless; but he who hath no need shall give account, why he took, and for what purpose, and coming under arrest shall be examined concerning what he did, and shall not go out thence until he pay the last farthing. But it hath been also said concerning this *matter*: Let thine alms sweat in thy hands, until thou knowest to whom thou shouldst give.

CHAP. II.—Now the second commandment of the teaching *is*: Thou shalt not kill, thou shalt not commit adultery, thou shalt not corrupt boys, thou shalt not

οὐ κλέψεις, οὐ μαγεύσεις, οὐ φαρμακεύσεις, οὐ
φονεύσεις τέκνον ἐν φθορᾷ οὐδὲ γεννηθὲν ἀπο-
κτενεῖς. Οὐκ ἐπιθυμήσεις τὰ τοῦ πλησίον,
οὐκ ἐπιορκήσεις, οὐ ψευδομαρτυρήσεις, οὐ κακο-
λογήσεις, οὐ μνησικακήσεις. Οὐκ ἔσῃ διγνώμων
οὐδὲ δίγλωσσος· παγὶς γὰρ θανάτου ἡ διγλωσ-
σία. Οὐκ ἔσται ὁ λόγος σου ψευδής, οὐ κενός,
ἀλλὰ μεμεστωμένος πράξει. Οὐκ ἔσῃ πλεονέκ-
της οὐδὲ ἅρπαξ οὐδὲ ὑποκριτὴς οὐδὲ κακοήθης
οὐδὲ ὑπερήφανος. Οὐ λήψῃ βουλὴν πονηρὰν
κατὰ τοῦ πλησίον σου. Οὐ μισήσεις πάντα ἄν-
θρωπον, ἀλλὰ οὓς μὲν ἐλέγξεις, περὶ δὲ ὧν προσ-
εύξῃ, οὓς δὲ ἀγαπήσεις ὑπὲρ τὴν ψυχήν σου.

Κεφ. γʹ. Τέκνον μου, φεῦγε ἀπὸ παντὸς πονηροῦ καὶ
ἀπὸ παντὸς ὁμοίου αὐτοῦ· Μὴ γίνου ὀργίλος·
ὁδηγεῖ γὰρ ἡ ὀργὴ πρὸς τὸν φόνον· μηδὲ ζηλω-
τὴς μηδὲ ἐριστικὸς μηδὲ θυμικός· ἐκ γὰρ τούτων ἁπάντων φόνοι γεννῶνται. Τέκνον μου, μὴ
γίνου ἐπιθυμητής· ὁδηγεῖ γὰρ ἡ ἐπιθυμία πρὸς
τὴν πορνείαν· μηδὲ αἰσχρολόγος μηδὲ ὑψηλόφ-
θαλμος· ἐκ γὰρ τούτων ἁπάντων μοιχεῖαι γεννῶνται. Τέκνον μου, μὴ γίνου οἰωνοσκόπος·
ἐπειδὴ ὁδηγεῖ εἰς τὴν εἰδωλολατρείαν· μηδὲ ἐπα-
οιδὸς μηδὲ μαθηματικὸς μηδὲ περικαθαίρων,

6

commit fornication, thou shalt not steal, thou shalt not practise magic, thou shalt not use sorcery, thou shalt not slay a child by abortion, nor what is begotten shalt thou destroy. Thou shalt not lust after the things of thy neighbor, thou shalt not forswear thyself, thou shalt not bear false witness, thou shalt not revile, thou shalt not bear malice. Thou shalt not be doubled-minded nor doubled-tongued ; for a snare of death is the double tongue. Thy speech shall not be false, nor empty, but filled with doing. Thou shalt not be covetous, nor rapacious, nor a hypocrite, nor malicious, nor arrogant. Thou shalt not take evil counsel against thy neighbor. Thou shalt hate no man, but some thou shalt reprove, and for some thou shalt pray, and some thou shalt love above thy life.

Chap. III.—My child, flee from every evil thing, and from everything like it. Be not inclined to anger, for anger leadeth to murder ; nor jealous, nor contentious, nor passionate ; for of all these murders are begotten. My child, become not lustful ; for lust leadeth to fornication ; nor foul-mouthed, nor lofty-eyed ; for of all these things adulteries are begotten. My child, become not an omen-watcher ; since it leadeth into idolatry ; nor an enchanter, nor an astrologer, nor a purifier, nor

7

μηδὲ θέλε αὐτὰ βλέπειν· ἐκ γὰρ τούτων ἁπάντων εἰδωλολατρεία γεννᾶται. Τέκνον μου, μὴ
γίνου ψεύστης· ἐπειδὴ ὁδηγεῖ τὸ ψεῦσμα εἰς
τὴν κλοπήν· μηδὲ φιλάργυρος μηδὲ κενόδοξος·
65 ἐκ γὰρ τούτων ἁπάντων κλοπαὶ γεννῶνται. Τέκνον μου, μὴ γίνου γόγγυσος· ἐπειδὴ ὁδηγεῖ εἰς τὴν
βλασφημίαν· μηδὲ αὐθάδης μηδὲ πονηρόφρων·
ἐκ γὰρ τούτων ἁπάντων βλασφημίαι γεννῶνται.
Ἴσθι δὲ πραΰς, ἐπεὶ οἱ πραεῖς κληρονομήσουσι
70 τὴν γῆν. Γίνου μακρόθυμος καὶ ἐλεήμων καὶ
ἄκακος καὶ ἡσύχιος καὶ ἀγαθὸς καὶ τρέμων τοὺς
λόγους διὰ παντός, οὓς ἤκουσας. Οὐκ ὑψώσεις
σεαυτὸν οὐδὲ δώσεις τῇ ψυχῇ σου θράσος. Οὐ
κολληθήσεται ἡ ψυχή σου μετὰ ὑψηλῶν, ἀλλὰ
75 μετὰ δικαίων καὶ ταπεινῶν ἀναστραφήσῃ. Τὰ
συμβαίνοντά σοι ἐνεργήματα ὡς ἀγαθὰ προσ-
δέξῃ, εἰδὼς ὅτι ἄτερ Θεοῦ οὐδὲν γίνεται.

Κεφ. δ΄. Τέκνον μου, τοῦ λαλοῦντός σοι τὸν λόγον τοῦ
Θεοῦ μνησθήσῃ νυκτὸς καὶ ἡμέρας, τιμήσεις δὲ
80 αὐτὸν ὡς Κύριον· ὅθεν γὰρ ἡ κυριότης λαλεῖται,
ἐκεῖ Κύριός ἐστιν. Ἐκζητήσεις δὲ καθ᾿ ἡμέραν
τὰ πρόσωπα τῶν ἁγίων, ἵνα ἐπαναπαύῃ τοῖς
λόγοις αὐτῶν. Οὐ ποθήσεις σχίσμα, εἰρηνεύ-
σεις δὲ μαχομένους· κρινεῖς δικαίως, οὐ λήψῃ

be willing to look upon these things; for of all these things idolatry is begotten. My child, become not a liar; since lying leads to theft; nor avaricious, nor vainglorious; for of all these things thefts are begotten. My child, become not a murmurer; since it leads to blasphemy; nor presumptuous, nor evil-minded; for of all these things blasphemies are begotten. But be meek, since the meek shall inherit the earth. Become long-suffering and pitiful and guileless and gentle and good, and tremble continually at the words which thou hast heard. Thou shalt not exalt thyself, nor permit over-boldness to thy soul. Thy soul shall not cleave to the high, but with the righteous and lowly thou shalt dwell. The things that befall thee accept as well-wrought, knowing that without God nothing occurs.

CHAP. IV.—My child, him that speaks to thee the word of God remember night and day, and thou shalt honor him as the Lord; for where that which pertaineth to the Lord is spoken there the Lord is. And thou shalt seek out daily the faces of the saints that thou mayst be refreshed by their words. Thou shalt not desire division, but shalt make peace between those who contend; thou

85 πρόσωπον ἐλέγξαι ἐπὶ παραπτώμασιν. Οὐ δι-
ψυχήσεις, πότερον ἔσται ἢ οὔ. Μὴ γίνου πρὸς
μὲν τὸ λαβεῖν ἐκτείνων τὰς χεῖρας, πρὸς δὲ τὸ
δοῦναι συσπῶν· ἐὰν ἔχῃς, διὰ τῶν χειρῶν σου
δώσεις λύτρωσιν ἁμαρτιῶν σου. Οὐ διστάσεις
90 δοῦναι οὐδὲ διδοὺς γογγύσεις· γνώσῃ γὰρ τίς
ἐστιν ὁ τοῦ μισθοῦ καλὸς ἀνταποδότης. Οὐκ
ἀποστραφήσῃ τὸν ἐνδεόμενον, συγκοινωνήσεις
δὲ πάντα τῷ ἀδελφῷ σου καὶ οὐκ ἐρεῖς ἴδια εἶναι·
εἰ γὰρ ἐν τῷ ἀθανάτῳ κοινωνοί ἐστε, πόσῳ
95 μᾶλλον ἐν τοῖς θνητοῖς; Οὐκ ἀρεῖς τὴν χεῖρά
σου ἀπὸ τοῦ υἱοῦ σου ἢ ἀπὸ τῆς θυγατρός σου,
ἀλλὰ ἀπὸ νεότητος διδάξεις τὸν φόβον τοῦ
Θεοῦ. Οὐκ ἐπιτάξεις δούλῳ σου ἢ παιδίσκῃ,
τοῖς ἐπὶ τὸν αὐτὸν Θεὸν ἐλπίζουσιν, ἐν πικρίᾳ
100 σου, μήποτε οὐ μὴ φοβηθήσονται τὸν ἐπ᾽ ἀμ-
φοτέροις Θεόν· οὐ γὰρ ἔρχεται κατὰ πρόσωπον
καλέσαι, ἀλλ᾽ ἐφ᾽ οὓς τὸ πνεῦμα ἡτοίμασεν.
Ὑμεῖς δὲ οἱ δοῦλοι ὑποταγήσεσθε τοῖς κυρίοις
ὑμῶν ὡς τύπῳ Θεοῦ ἐν αἰσχύνῃ καὶ φόβῳ.
105 Μισήσεις πᾶσαν ὑπόκρισιν καὶ πᾶν ὃ μὴ ἀρεσ-
τὸν τῷ Κυρίῳ. Οὐ μὴ ἐγκαταλίπῃς ἐντολὰς
Κυρίου, φυλάξεις δὲ ἃ παρέλαβες, μήτε προστι-
θεὶς μήτε ἀφαιρῶν. Ἐν ἐκκλησίᾳ ἐξομολογήσῃ
τὰ παραπτώματά σου, καὶ οὐ προσελεύσῃ ἐπὶ

shalt judge justly, thou shalt not respect persons in convicting for transgressions. Thou shalt not hesitate whether it shall be or not. Become not *one who* for taking stretches out the hands, but for giving draws them in; if thou hast *anything*, by thy hands thou shalt give a ransom for thy sins. Thou shalt not hesitate to give, nor when giving shalt thou murmur, for thou shalt know who is the good dispenser of the recompense. Thou shalt not turn away the needy, but shalt share all things with thy brother, and shalt not say they are thine own; for if ye are partners in that which is imperishable, how much more in the perishable things? Thou shalt not take off thy hand from thy son and from thy daughter, but from youth thou shalt teach *them* the fear of God. Thou shalt not lay commands in thy bitterness upon thy slave or handmaid, who hope in the same God, lest they perchance shalt not fear the God who is over *you* both; for he cometh not to call *men* according to the appearance, but to those whom the Spirit hath made ready. And ye, slaves, ye shall be subject to your lords, as to God's image, in modesty and fear. Thou shalt hate every hypocrisy, and whatever is not pleasing to the Lord. Thou shalt by no means forsake the Lord's commandments, but shalt guard what thou hast received, neither adding to it nor taking from it. In the church

110 προσευχήν σου ἐν συνειδήσει πονηρᾷ. Αὕτη
ἐστὶν ἡ ὁδὸς τῆς ζωῆς.

Κεφ. ε΄. Ἡ δὲ τοῦ θανάτου ὁδός ἐστιν αὕτη· πρῶτον
πάντων πονηρά ἐστι καὶ κατάρας μεστή· φόνοι,
μοιχεῖαι, ἐπιθυμίαι, πορνεῖαι, κλοπαί, εἰδωλο-
115 λατρεῖαι, μαγεῖαι, φαρμακεῖαι, ἁρπαγαί, ψευδο-
μαρτυρίαι, ὑποκρίσεις, διπλοκαρδία, δόλος, ὑπερ-
ηφανία, κακία, αὐθάδεια, πλεονεξία, αἰσχρολο-
γία, ζηλοτυπία, θρασύτης, ὕψος, ἀλαζονεία·
διῶκται ἀγαθῶν, μισοῦντες ἀλήθειαν, ἀγαπῶν-
120 τες ψεῦδος, οὐ γινώσκοντες μισθὸν δικαιο-
σύνης, οὐ κολλώμενοι ἀγαθῷ οὐδὲ κρίσει δι-
καίᾳ, ἀγρυπνοῦντες οὐκ εἰς τὸ ἀγαθόν, ἀλλ᾽
εἰς τὸ πονηρόν· ὧν μακρὰν πραΰτης καὶ ὑπο-
μονή, μάταια ἀγαπῶντες, διώκοντες ἀνταπό-
125 δομα, οὐκ ἐλεοῦντες πτωχόν, οὐ πονοῦντες ἐπὶ
καταπονουμένῳ, οὐ γινώσκοντες τὸν ποιήσαντα
αὐτούς, φονεῖς τέκνων, φθορεῖς πλάσματος Θεοῦ,
ἀποστρεφόμενοι τὸν ἐνδεόμενον, καταπονοῦντες
τὸν θλιβόμενον, πλουσίων παράκλητοι, πενή-
130 των ἄνομοι κριταί, πανθαμάρτητοι· ρυσθείητε,
τέκνα, ἀπὸ τούτων ἁπάντων.

Κεφ. ς΄. Ὅρα μή τις σε πλανήσῃ ἀπὸ ταύτης τῆς ὁδοῦ
τῆς διδαχῆς, ἐπεὶ παρεκτὸς Θεοῦ σε διδάσκει.

thou shalt confess thy transgressions, and shalt not come forward for thy prayer with an evil conscience. This is the way of life.

Chap. V.—Now the way of death is this: first of all it is evil, and full of curse; murders, adulteries, lusts, fornications, thefts, idolatries, magic arts, sorceries, robberies, false testimonies, hypocrisies, duplicity, craft, arrogance, vice, presumptuousness, greed, foul speech, jealousy, over-boldness, loftiness, pretence; persecutors of the good, hating truth, loving falsehood, knowing not the reward of righteousness, not cleaving to *that which is* good nor to righteous judgment, on the watch not for good but for evil; far from whom are meekness and patience, loving vanities, pursuing revenge, not pitying a poor *man*, not laboring for the distressed, not knowing him that made them, murderers of children, destroyers of the image of God, turning away the needy, oppressing the afflicted, advocates of the rich, lawless judges of the poor, universal sinners: may ye be delivered, children, from all these.

Chap. VI.—See that no one lead thee astray from this way of the teaching, because apart from God does

135   Εἰ μὲν γὰρ δύνασαι βαστάσαι ὅλον τὸν ζυγὸν
τοῦ Κυρίου, τέλειος ἔσῃ· εἰ δ' οὐ δύνασαι, ὃ δύνῃ
τοῦτο ποίει. Περὶ δὲ τῆς βρώσεως, ὃ δύνασαι
βάστασον· ἀπὸ δὲ τοῦ εἰδωλοθύτου λίαν πρόσ-
εχε· λατρεία γάρ ἐστι Θεῶν νεκρῶν.

Κεφ. ζ'. Περὶ δὲ τοῦ βαπτίσματος, οὕτω βαπτίσατε·
140   ταῦτα πάντα προειπόντες, βαπτίσατε εἰς τὸ
ὄνομα τοῦ Πατρὸς καὶ τοῦ Υἱοῦ καὶ τοῦ ἁγίου
Πνεύματος ἐν ὕδατι ζῶντι. Ἐὰν δὲ μὴ ἔχῃς
ὕδωρ ζῶν, εἰς ἄλλο ὕδωρ βάπτισον· εἰ δ' οὐ
δύνασαι ἐν ψυχρῷ, ἐν θερμῷ. Ἐὰν δε ἀμφότερα
145   μὴ ἔχῃς, ἔκχεον εἰς τὴν κεφαλὴν τρὶς ὕδωρ εἰς
ὄνομα Πατρὸς καὶ Υἱοῦ καὶ ἁγίου Πνεύματος.
Πρὸ δὲ τοῦ βαπτίσματος προνηστευσάτω ὁ βαπ-
τίζων καὶ ὁ βαπτιζόμενος καὶ εἴ τινες ἄλλοι δύ-
νανται· κελεύσεις δὲ νηστεῦσαι τὸν βαπτιζό-
150   μενον πρὸ μιᾶς ἢ δύο.

Κεφ. η'. Αἱ δὲ νηστεῖαι ὑμῶν μὴ ἔστωσαν μετὰ τῶν
ὑποκριτῶν· νηστεύουσι γὰρ δευτέρᾳ σαββά-
των καὶ πέμπτῃ· ὑμεῖς δὲ νηστεύσατε τετ-
ράδα καὶ παρασκευήν. Μηδὲ προσεύχεσθε
155   ὡς οἱ ὑποκριταί, ἀλλ' ὡς ἐκέλευσεν ὁ Κύριος
ἐν τῷ εὐαγγελίῳ αὐτοῦ, οὕτω προσεύχεσθε·

he teach thee. For if thou art able to bear the whole yoke of the Lord, thou shalt be perfect; but if thou art not able, what thou art able, that do. And concerning food, what thou art able, bear; but of that offered to idols, beware exceedingly; for it is a worship of dead gods.

CHAP. VII.—Now concerning baptism, thus baptize ye: having first uttered all these things, baptize into the name of the Father, and of the Son, and of the Holy Spirit, in running water. But if thou hast not running water, baptize in other water; and if thou canst not in cold, *then* in warm. But if thou hast neither, pour water upon the head thrice, into the name of Father and Son and Holy Spirit. But before the baptism let the baptizer and the baptized fast, and whatever others can; but the baptized thou shalt command to fast for two or three days before.

CHAP. VIII.—But let not your fastings be appointed in common with the hypocrites; for they fast on the second day of the week and on the fifth; but do ye fast during the fourth, and the preparation *day*. Nor pray ye like the hypocrites, but as the Lord commanded in his

Πάτερ ἡμῶν ὁ ἐν τῷ οὐρανῷ, ἁγιασθήτω τὸ
ὄνομά σου, ἐλθέτω ἡ βασιλεία σου, γενη-
θήτω τὸ θέλημά σου ὡς ἐν οὐρανῷ καὶ ἐπὶ γῆς·
160 τὸν ἄρτον ἡμῶν τὸν ἐπιούσιον δὸς ἡμῖν σήμε-
ρον καὶ ἄφες ἡμῖν τὴν ὀφειλὴν ἡμῶν ὡς καὶ
ἡμεῖς ἀφίεμεν τοῖς ὀφειλέταις ἡμῶν, καὶ μὴ
εἰσενέγκῃς ἡμᾶς εἰς πειρασμόν, ἀλλὰ ῥῦσαι ἡμᾶς
ἀπὸ τοῦ πονηροῦ· ὅτι σοῦ ἐστιν ἡ δύναμις καὶ ἡ
165 δόξα εἰς τοὺς αἰῶνας. Τρὶς τῆς ἡμέρας οὕτω
προσεύχεσθε.

Κεφ. θ´. Περὶ δὲ τῆς εὐχαριστίας, οὕτως εὐχαριστήσατε·
πρῶτον περὶ τοῦ ποτηρίου· Εὐχαριστοῦμέν σοι,
Πάτερ ἡμῶν, ὑπὲρ τῆς ἁγίας ἀμπέλου Δαβὶδ
170 τοῦ παιδός σου, ἧς ἐγνώρισας ἡμῖν διὰ Ἰησοῦ
τοῦ παιδός σου· σοὶ ἡ δόξα εἰς τοὺς αἰῶνας. Περὶ
δὲ τοῦ κλάσματος· Εὐχαριστοῦμέν σοι, Πάτερ
ἡμῶν, ὑπὲρ τῆς ζωῆς καὶ γνώσεως, ἧς ἐγνώρισας
ἡμῖν διὰ Ἰησοῦ τοῦ παιδός σου· σοὶ ἡ δόξα εἰς
175 τοὺς αἰῶνας. Ὥσπερ ἦν τοῦτο κλάσμα διεσκορ-
πισμένον ἐπάνω τῶν ὀρέων καὶ συναχθὲν ἐγέ-
νετο ἕν, οὕτω συναχθήτω σου ἡ ἐκκλησία ἀπὸ
τῶν περάτων τῆς γῆς εἰς τὴν σὴν βασιλείαν·
ὅτι σοῦ ἐστιν ἡ δοξα καὶ ἡ δύναμις διὰ Ἰησοῦ
180 Χριστοῦ εἰς τοὺς αἰῶνας. Μηδεὶς δὲ φαγέτω

16

gospel, thus pray: Our Father who art in heaven, Hallowed be thy name, thy kingdom come, thy will be done, as in heaven, so on earth; our daily bread give us to-day, and forgive us our debt as we also forgive our debtors, and bring us not into temptation, but deliver us from the evil *one*; for thine is the power and the glory forever. Three times in the day pray ye thus.

Chap. IX.—Now concerning the Eucharist, thus give thanks; first, concerning the cup: We thank thee, our Father, for the holy vine of David thy servant, which thou hast made known to us through Jesus thy servant; to thee be the glory forever. And concerning the broken *bread*: We thank thee, our Father, for the life and the knowledge which thou hast made known to us through Jesus thy servant; to thee be the glory forever. Just as this broken *bread* was scattered over the hills and having been gathered together became one, so let thy church be gathered together from the ends of the earth into thy kingdom; for thine is the glory and the power through Jesus Christ forever. But let no one eat

μηδὲ πιέτω ἀπὸ τῆς εὐχαριστίας ὑμῶν, ἀλλ᾿ οἱ βαπτισθέντες εἰς ὄνομα Κυρίου· καὶ γὰρ περὶ τούτου εἴρηκεν ὁ Κύριος· Μὴ δῶτε τὸ ἅγιον τοῖς κυσί.

185 Κεφ. ι´. Μετὰ δὲ τὸ ἐμπλησθῆναι οὕτως εὐχαριστήσατε· Εὐχαριστοῦμέν σοι, Πάτερ ἅγιε, ὑπὲρ τοῦ ἁγίου ὀνόματός σου, οὗ κατεσκήνωσας ἐν ταῖς καρδίαις ἡμῶν, καὶ ὑπὲρ τῆς γνώσεως καὶ πίστεως καὶ ἀθανασίας· ἧς ἐγνώρισας ἡμῖν διὰ 190 Ἰησοῦ τοῦ παιδός σου· σοὶ ἡ δόξα εἰς τοὺς αἰῶνας. Σύ, δέσποτα παντοκράτορ, ἔκτισας τὰ πάντα ἕνεκεν τοῦ ὀνόματός σου, τροφήν τε καὶ ποτὸν ἔδωκας τοῖς ἀνθρώποις εἰς ἀπόλαυσιν ἵνα σοι εὐχαριστήσωσιν, ἡμῖν δὲ ἐχαρίσω πνευ- 195 ματικὴν τροφὴν καὶ ποτὸν καὶ ζωὴν αἰώνιον διὰ τοῦ παιδός σου. Πρὸ πάντων εὐχαριστοῦμέν σοι ὅτι δυνατὸς εἶ· σοὶ ἡ δόξα εἰς τοὺς αἰῶνας. Μνήσθητι, Κύριε, τῆς ἐκκλησίας σου τοῦ ῥύσασθαι αὐτὴν ἀπὸ παντὸς πονηροῦ καὶ τελειῶσαι 200 αὐτὴν ἐν τῇ ἀγάπῃ σου, καὶ σύναξον αὐτὴν ἀπὸ τῶν τεσσάρων ἀνέμων, τὴν ἁγιασθεῖσαν εἰς τὴν σὴν βασιλείαν, ἣν ἡτοίμασας αὐτῇ· ὅτι σοῦ ἐστιν ἡ δύναμις καὶ ἡ δόξα εἰς τοὺς αἰῶνας. Ἐλθέτω χάρις καὶ παρελθέτω ὁ κόσμος οὗτος.

or drink of your Eucharist, except those baptized into the Lord's name; for in regard to this the Lord hath said: Give not that which is holy to the dogs.

CHAP. X.—Now after ye are filled thus do ye give thanks: We thank thee, holy Father, for thy holy name, which thou hast caused to dwell in our hearts, and for the knowledge and faith and immortality which thou hast made known to us through Jesus thy servant; to thee be the glory forever. Thou, Almighty Master, didst create all things for thy name's sake; both food and drink thou didst give to men for enjoyment, in order that they might give thanks to thee; but to us thou hast graciously given spiritual food and drink and eternal life through thy servant. Before all things, we thank thee that thou art powerful; to thee be the glory forever. Remember, Lord, thy church, to deliver it from every evil and to make it perfect in thy love, and gather it from the four winds, it, the sanctified, into thy kingdom, which thou hast prepared for it; for thine is the power and the glory forever. Let grace come and let this world pass away. Hosanna to

205 Ὡσαννὰ τῷ υἱῷ Δαβίδ. Εἴ τις ἅγιός ἐστιν, ἐρ-
χέσθω· εἴ τις οὐκ ἔστι, μετανοείτω· μαραναθά.
Ἀμήν. Τοῖς δὲ προφήταις ἐπιτρέπετε εὐχα-
ριστεῖν ὅσα θέλουσιν.

Κεφ. ια΄. Ὃς ἂν οὖν ἐλθὼν διδάξῃ ὑμᾶς ταῦτα πάντα,
210 τὰ προειρημένα, δέξασθε αὐτόν· ἐὰν δὲ αὐτὸς
ὁ διδάσκων στραφεὶς διδάσκῃ ἄλλην διδαχὴν εἰς
τὸ καταλῦσαι, μὴ αὐτοῦ ἀκούσητε· εἰς δὲ τὸ
προσθεῖναι δικαιοσύνην καὶ γνῶσιν Κυρίου,
δέξασθε αὐτὸν ὡς Κύριον. Περὶ δὲ τῶν ἀποσ-
215 τόλων καὶ προφητῶν κατὰ τὸ δόγμα τοῦ εὐαγ-
γελίου, οὕτω ποιήσατε. Πᾶς δὲ ἀπόστολος
ἐρχόμενος πρὸς ὑμᾶς δεχθήτω ὡς Κύριος· οὐ
μενεῖ δὲ ἡμέραν μίαν· ἐὰν δὲ ᾖ χρεία, καὶ τὴν
ἄλλην· τρεῖς δὲ ἐὰν μείνῃ, ψευδοπροφήτης
220 ἐστίν. Ἐξερχόμενος δὲ ὁ ἀπόστολος μηδὲν λαμ-
βανέτω εἰμὴ ἄρτον ἕως οὗ αὐλισθῇ· ἐὰν δὲ ἀρ-
γύριον αἰτῇ, ψευδοπροφήτης ἐστί. Καὶ πάντα
προφήτην λαλοῦντα ἐν πνεύματι οὐ πειράσετε
οὐδὲ διακρινεῖτε· πᾶσα γὰρ ἁμαρτία ἀφεθή-
225 σεται, αὕτη δὲ ἡ ἁμαρτία οὐκ ἀφεθήσεται. Οὐ
πᾶς δὲ ὁ λαλῶν ἐν πνεύματι προφήτης ἐστίν,
ἀλλ᾽ ἐὰν ἔχῃ τοὺς τρόπους Κυρίου. Ἀπὸ οὖν
τῶν τρόπων γνωσθήσεται ὁ ψευδοπροφήτης καὶ

the son of David! Whoever is holy, let him come; whoever is not, let him repent. Maranatha. Amen. But permit the prophets to give thanks as much as they will.

CHAP. XI.—Now whoever cometh and teacheth you all these things, before spoken, receive him; but if the teacher himself turn aside and teach another teaching, so as to overthrow *this*, do not hear him; but *if he teach* so as to promote righteousness and knowledge of the Lord, receive him as the Lord. But in regard to the apostles and prophets, according to the ordinance of the gospel, so do ye. And every apostle who cometh to you, let him be received as the Lord; but he shall not remain *more than* one day; if, however, there be need, then the next *day*; but if he remain three days, he is a false prophet. But when the apostle departeth, let him take nothing except bread enough till he lodge *again*; but if he ask money, he is a false prophet. And every prophet who speaketh in the spirit, ye shall not try nor judge; for every sin shall be forgiven, but this sin shall not be forgiven. But not every one that speaketh in the spirit is a prophet, but *only* if he have the ways of the Lord. So from their ways shall the false prophet

ὁ προφήτης. Καὶ πᾶς προφήτης ὁρίζων τρά-
230 πεζαν ἐν πνεύματι, οὐ φάγεται ἀπ᾽ αὐτῆς, εἰδὲ
μήγε ψευδοπροφήτης ἐστί· πᾶς δὲ προφήτης
διδάσκων τὴν ἀλήθειαν, εἰ ἃ διδάσκει οὐ ποιεῖ,
ψευδοπροφήτης ἐστί. Πᾶς δὲ προφήτης δεδοκι-
μασμένος, ἀληθινός, ποιῶν εἰς μυστήριον κοσμι-
235 κὸν ἐκκλησίας, μὴ διδάσκων δὲ ποιεῖν ὅσα αὐτὸς
ποιεῖ, οὐ κριθήσεται ἐφ᾽ ὑμῶν· μετὰ Θεοῦ γὰρ
ἔχει τὴν κρίσιν· ὡσαύτως γὰρ ἐποίησαν καὶ οἱ
ἀρχαῖοι προφῆται. Ὃς δ᾽ἂν εἴπῃ ἐν πνεύματι·
Δός μοι ἀργύρια ἢ ἕτερά τινα, οὐκ ἀκούσεσθε
240 αὐτοῦ· ἐὰν δὲ περὶ ἄλλων ὑστερούντων εἴπῃ
δοῦναι, μηδεὶς αὐτὸν κρινέτω.

Κεφ. ιβ'. Πᾶς δὲ ὁ ἐρχόμενος ἐν ὀνόματι Κυρίου δεχθήτω, ἔπειτα δὲ δοκιμάσαντες αὐτὸν γνώσεσθε·
σύνεσιν γὰρ ἕξετε δεξιὰν καὶ ἀριστεράν. Εἰμὲν
245 παρόδιός ἐστιν ὁ ἐρχόμενος, βοηθεῖτε αὐτῷ ὅσον
δύνασθε· οὐ μενεῖ δὲ πρὸς ὑμᾶς εἰ μὴ δύο ἢ
τρεῖς ἡμέρας, ἐὰν ᾖ ἀνάγκη. Εἰ δὲ θέλει πρὸς
ὑμᾶς καθῆσαι, τεχνίτης ὤν, ἐργαζέσθω καὶ
φαγέτω· εἰ δὲ οὐκ ἔχει τέχνην, κατὰ τὴν σύνεσιν
250 ὑμῶν προνοήσατε, πῶς μὴ ἀργὸς μεθ᾽ ὑμῶν ζήσε-
ται χριστιανός. Εἰ δ᾽ οὐ θέλει οὕτω ποιεῖν, χρισ-
τέμπορός ἐστι· προσέχετε ἀπὸ τῶν τοιούτων.

22

and the prophet be known. And no prophet who orders a meal, in the spirit, eateth of it, unless indeed he is a false prophet; and every prophet who teacheth the truth, if he do not that which he teacheth, is a false prophet. But every prophet, proved, true, acting with a view to the mystery of the church on earth, but not teaching *others* to do all that he himself doeth, shall not be judged among you; for with God he hath his judgment; for so did the ancient prophets also. But whoever, in the spirit, says: Give me money, or something else, ye shall not hear him; but if for others in need, he bids *you* give, let no one judge him.

Chap. XII.—But let every one that cometh in the Lord's name be received, but afterward ye shall test and know him; for ye shall have understanding, right and left. If he who comes is a traveller, help him as much as ye can; but he shall not remain with you, unless for two or three days, if there be necessity. But if he will take up his abode among you, being an artisan, let him work and so eat; but if he have no trade, provide, according to your understanding, that no idler live with you as a Christian. But if he will not act according to this, he is one who makes gain out of Christ; beware of such.

Κεφ. ιγ'. Πᾶς δὲ προφήτης ἀληθινός, θέλων καθῆσαι
πρὸς ὑμᾶς, ἄξιός ἐστι τῆς τροφῆς αὐτοῦ. Ὡσαύ-
255 τως διδάσκαλος ἀληθινός ἐστιν ἄξιος καὶ αὐ-
τός, ὥσπερ ὁ ἐργάτης, τῆς τροφῆς αὐτοῦ. Πᾶσαν οὖν ἀπαρχὴν γεννημάτων ληνοῦ καὶ ἅλωνος,
βοῶν τε καὶ προβάτων λαβὼν δώσεις τοῖς προ-
φήταις· αὐτοὶ γάρ εἰσιν οἱ ἀρχιερεῖς ὑμῶν.
260 Ἐὰν δὲ μὴ ἔχητε προφήτην, δότε τοῖς πτωχοῖς.
Ἐὰν σιτίαν ποιῇς, τὴν ἀπαρχὴν λαβὼν δὸς κατὰ
τὴν ἐντολήν. Ὡσαύτως κεράμιον οἴνου ἢ ἐλαίου
ἀνοίξας, τὴν ἀπαρχὴν λαβὼν δὸς τοῖς προφήταις·
ἀργυρίου δὲ καὶ ἱματισμοῦ καὶ παντὸς κτήματος
265 λαβὼν τὴν ἀπαρχὴν ὡς ἄν σοι δόξῃ, δὸς κατὰ
τὴν ἐντολήν.

Κεφ. ιδ'. Κατὰ κυριακὴν δὲ Κυρίου συναχθέντες κλά-
σατε ἄρτον καὶ εὐχαριστήσατε προσεξομολογη-
σάμενοι τὰ παραπτώματα ὑμῶν, ὅπως καθαρὰ
270 ἡ θυσία ὑμῶν ᾖ. Πᾶς δὲ ἔχων τὴν ἀμφιβολίαν
μετὰ τοῦ ἑταίρου αὐτοῦ μὴ συνελθέτω ὑμῖν, ἕως
οὗ διαλλαγῶσιν, ἵνα μὴ κοινωθῇ ἡ θυσία ὑμῶν·
αὕτη γάρ ἐστιν ἡ ῥηθεῖσα ὑπὸ Κυρίου· Ἐν
παντὶ τόπῳ καὶ χρόνῳ προσφέρειν μοι θυσίαν
275 καθαράν· ὅτι βασιλεὺς μέγας εἰμί, λέγει Κύριος, καὶ τὸ ὄνομά μου θαυμαστὸν ἐν τοῖς ἔθνεσι.

24

CHAP. XIII.—But every true prophet who will settle among you is worthy of his support. Likewise a true teacher, he also is worthy, like the workman, of his support. Every firstfruit, then, of the products of wine-press and threshing-floor, of oxen and of sheep, thou shalt take and give to the prophets; for they are your high-priests. But if ye have no prophet, give *it* to the poor. If thou makest a baking of bread, take the first *of it* and give according to the commandment. In like manner when thou openest a jar of wine or oil, take the first *of it* and give to the prophets; and of money and clothing and every possession take the first, as seems right to thee, and give according to the commandment.

CHAP. XIV.—But on the Lord's day do ye assemble and break bread, and give thanks, after confessing your transgressions, in order that your sacrifice may be pure. But every one that hath controversy with his friend, let him not come together with you, until they be reconciled, that your sacrifice may not be profaned. For this is that which was spoken by the Lord: At every place and time, bring me a pure sacrifice; for a great king am I, saith the Lord, and my name is marvellous among the nations.

Κεφ. ιε'. Χειροτονήσατε οὖν ἑαυτοῖς ἐπισκόπους καὶ
διακόνους ἀξίους τοῦ Κυρίου, ἄνδρας πραεῖς καὶ
ἀφιλαργύρους καὶ ἀληθεῖς καὶ δεδοκιμασμένους·

280 ὑμῖν γὰρ λειτουργοῦσι καὶ αὐτοὶ τὴν λειτουργί-
αν τῶν προφητῶν καὶ διδασκάλων. Μὴ οὖν
ὑπερίδητε αὐτούς· αὐτοὶ γάρ εἰσιν οἱ τετιμημέ-
νοι ὑμῶν μετὰ τῶν προφητῶν καὶ διδασκάλων.

 Ἐλέγχετε δὲ ἀλλήλους μὴ ἐν ὀργῇ, ἀλλ' ἐν
285 εἰρήνῃ, ὡς ἔχετε ἐν τῷ εὐαγγελίῳ· καὶ παντὶ
ἀστοχοῦντι κατὰ τοῦ ἑτέρου μηδεὶς λαλείτω μηδὲ
παρ' ὑμῶν ἀκουέτω, ἕως οὗ μετανοήσῃ. Τὰς δὲ
εὐχὰς ὑμῶν καὶ τὰς ἐλεημοσύνας καὶ πάσας τὰς
πράξεις οὕτω ποιήσατε, ὡς ἔχετε ἐν τῷ εὐαγγε-
290 λίῳ τοῦ Κυρίου ἡμῶν.

Κεφ. ιϛ'. Γρηγορεῖτε ὑπὲρ τῆς ζωῆς ὑμῶν· οἱ λύχνοι
ὑμῶν μὴ σβεσθήτωσαν, καὶ αἱ ὀσφύες ὑμῶν μὴ
ἐκλυέσθωσαν, ἀλλὰ γίνεσθε ἕτοιμοι· οὐ γὰρ
οἴδατε τὴν ὥραν, ἐν ᾗ ὁ Κύριος ἡμῶν ἔρχεται.
295 Πυκνῶς δὲ συναχθήσεσθε ζητοῦντες τὰ ἀνήκον-
τα ταῖς ψυχαῖς ὑμῶν· οὐ γὰρ ὠφελήσει ὑμᾶς
ὁ πᾶς χρόνος τῆς πίστεως ὑμῶν, ἐὰν μὴ ἐν τῷ
ἐσχάτῳ καιρῷ τελειωθῆτε. Ἐν γὰρ ταῖς ἐσχά-
ταις ἡμέραις πληθυνθήσονται οἱ ψευδοπροφῆται
300 καὶ οἱ φθορεῖς καὶ στραφήσονται τὰ πρόβατα

CHAP. XV.—Now appoint for yourselves bishops and deacons worthy of the Lord, men meek and not avaricious, and upright and proved; for they, too, render you the service of the prophets and teachers. Despise them not, therefore; for they are the ones who are honored of you, together with the prophets and teachers.

And reprove one another, not in anger, but in peace, as ye have *it* in the gospel; and to every one who erreth against another, let no one speak, nor let him hear *anything* from you, until he repent. But your prayers and your alms and all your deeds so do ye, as ye have *it* in the gospel of our Lord.

CHAP. XVI.—Watch for your life's sake; let your lamps not go out, and your loins not be relaxed, but be ready; for ye know not the hour in which our Lord cometh. But ye shall come together often, and seek the things which befit your souls; for the whole time of your faith *thus far* will not profit you, if ye do not become perfect in the last time. For in the last days the false prophets and the corruptors shall be multiplied, and the sheep shall be turned into wolves, and love

εἰς λύκους καὶ ἡ ἀγάπη στραφήσεται εἰς μῖσος·
αὐξανούσης γὰρ τῆς ἀνομίας, μισήσουσιν ἀλλήλους καὶ διώξουσι καὶ παραδώσουσι, καὶ τότε
φανήσεται ὁ κοσμοπλάνος ὡς υἱὸς Θεοῦ καὶ ποι-
305 ήσει σημεῖα καὶ τέρατα, καὶ ἡ γῆ παραδοθήσε-
ται εἰς χεῖρας αὐτοῦ, καὶ ποιήσει ἀθέμιτα, ἃ
οὐδέποτε γέγονεν ἐξ αἰῶνος. Τότε ἥξει ἡ κτίσις
τῶν ἀνθρώπων εἰς τὴν πύρωσιν τῆς δοκιμασίας
καὶ σκανδαλισθήσονται πολλοὶ καὶ ἀπολοῦνται,
310 οἱ δὲ ὑπομείναντες ἐν τῇ πίστει αὐτῶν σωθή-
σονται ὑπ᾽ αὐτοῦ τοῦ καταθέματος. Καὶ τότε
φανήσεται τὰ σημεῖα τῆς ἀληθείας· πρῶτον,
σημεῖον ἐκπετάσεως ἐν οὐρανῷ, εἶτα σημεῖον
φωνῆς σάλπιγγος καὶ τὸ τρίτον ἀνάστασις νε-
315 κρῶν· οὐ πάντων δέ, ἀλλ᾽ ὡς ἐρρέθη· Ἥξει ὁ
Κύριος καὶ πάντες οἱ ἅγιοι μετ᾽ αὐτοῦ. Τότε
ὄψεται ὁ κόσμος τὸν Κύριον ἐρχόμενον ἐπάνω
τῶν νεφελῶν τοῦ οὐρανοῦ.

shall be turned into hate; for when lawlessness increaseth they shall hate one another, and shall persecute and shall deliver up, and then shall appear the world-deceiver as the Son of God, and shall do signs and wonders, and the earth shall be given into his hands, and he shall commit iniquities which have never yet been done since the beginning. Then all created men shall come into the fire of trial, and many shall be made to stumble and shall perish. But they that endure in their faith shall be saved from this curse. And then shall appear the signs of the truth; first the sign of an opening in heaven, then the sign of the trumpet's sound, and thirdly, the resurrection of the dead; yet not of all, but as it hath been said: The Lord will come and all the saints with him. Then shall the world see the Lord coming upon the clouds of heaven.

USE OF THE HOLY SCRIPTURES IN THE "TEACHING."[1]

OLD TESTAMENT.

	LINE.		LINE.
*Deut. 5 : 17–19	35 f.	*Sirach 4 : 31	86 f.
*Tobit 4 : 15	7 f.	Zech. 14 : 5	315 f.
*Sirach 2 : 4	75 f.	Mal. 1 : 11, 14	273 f.
*Sirach 4 : 5	91 f.		

NEW TESTAMENT.

	LINE.		LINE.
*Matt. 5 : 5	69 f.	*Matt. 24 : 3-4	298 f.
*Matt. 5 : 22	284 f.	*Matt. 24 : 24–31	313 f.
*Matt. 5 : 26	30 f.	*Matt. 24 : 31	200 f.
*Matt. 5 : 39-48	16 f.	*Matt. 24 : 42, 44	291 f.
Matt. 6 : 5–13	155 f.	Matt 28 : 19	140 f.
*Matt. 6 and 7	289	*Luke 6 : 27–35	10
Matt. 7 : 6	183 f.	*Luke 9 : 1–6	215 f.
*Matt. 7 : 15–23	215 f.	*Luke 10 : 4–21	215 f.
*Matt. 10 : 5–12	215 f.	Luke 11 : 2–4	155 f.
*Matt. 10 : 10	256	*Luke 11 and 12	289 f.
*Matt. 12 : 31	224 f.	*Luke 12 : 35	291 f.
*Matt. 18 : 15–17	284	*Acts 4 : 32	92 f.
*Matt. 18 : 21–35	284	*Eph. 6 : 5, 9	103 f.
Matt. 21 : 9	205	*1 Thess. 5 : 22	50 f.
Matt. 22 : 27–39	5 f.	*1 Pet. 2 : 11	15 f.

[1] This table is that of Bryennios, who adds: " By this sign [*] are distinguished the passages which are not verbally cited in the 'Teaching,' and those to which the 'Teaching' simply refers, with the words, 'As the Lord commanded in the gospel.'" —EDS.

NOTES.

THE TITLE.

Another title is Διδαχὴ κυρίου διὰ τῶν δώδεκα Ἀποστόλων, "Teaching of the Lord through the Twelve Apostles." Athanasius also calls it διδαχή. But Eusebius (Hist. iii. 25) uses the plural, διδαχαί. And Clement of Alexandria cites it as γραφή.

CHAP. I.

P. 2, l. 8.—"do not to another"] The Golden Rule occurs both here and in the Apostolic Constitutions (vii. 2), in a negative form, as in the teachings of Confucius.

P. 2, l. 11.—"fast for them that persecute you"] The emphasis put upon fasting, here and elsewhere in this document, is no sign of Montanism, since fasting was much emphasized in the early Church, and Montanism itself was, in this respect, only an exaggeration of common usage.

P. 4, l. 15.—"ye shall have no enemy"] Suggested, apparently, by 1 Pet. iii. 13, "And who is he that will harm you, if ye be zealous of that which is good?"

P. 4, l. 22.—"for indeed thou canst not"] Because Christians were forbidden to "go to law before the unrighteous," 1 Cor. vi. 1.

P. 4, 1. 32.—"Let thine alms sweat in thy hands, until thou knowest to whom thou shouldst give"] A very graphic injunction of carefulness in giving.

CHAP. II.

P. 4, 1. 36.—"thou shalt not corrupt boys"] The παιδεραστία of Classic writers, referred to by Paul in Rom. i. 27.

P. 6, 1. 38.—"by abortion"] Another heathen abomination.

P. 6, 1. 42, 43.—διγλωσσία] This noun does not occur in Classic Greek, nor in the New Testament, but is found, together with the entire sentence in which it here stands, in the Epistle of Barnabas, Chap. xix. There are many other correspondences between that epistle and the present document.

P. 6, 1. 44.—"filled with doing"] *i.e.*, works, deeds, as in Matt. xvi. 27.

CHAP. III.

P. 6, 1. 60.—"nor a purifier"] Referring to some kind of superstitious lustration, perhaps by fire, as in Lev. xviii. 21; Deut. xviii. 10.

CHAP. IV.

P. 10, 1. 87.—"for taking stretches out the hands, but for giving draws them in"] Graphic description of taking and giving.

P. 10, 1. 88.—"by thy hands thou shalt give a ransom for thy sins"] Beneficence is better than sacrifice. See Prov. xvi. 6, "By mercy and truth iniquity is purged."

P. 10, 1. 98.—"thy slave"] As in the New Testament, so here, the relation of master and slave is not denounced, but regulated.

CHAP. V.

This catalogue of evil things pertaining to the "way of death," reflects only too faithfully the dreadful corruption of the ancient civilization.

CHAP. VI.

P. 14, l. 136.—"And concerning food, what thou art able, bear"] Nothing is unclean of itself, as Paul says in Rom. xiv. 14. And again in 1 Tim. iv. 4, "For every creature of God is good, and nothing is to be rejected, if it be received with thanksgiving."

CHAP. VII.

P. 14, l. 139.—"Now, concerning baptism . . . in running water"] ἐν ὕδατι ζῶντι, literally "in living water," water in motion, either as in a fountain, or as in a stream. A picture in the Catacomb of St. Callixtus, dating from about the year 200 A.D., represents a youth standing ankle-deep in water, and receiving baptism by the pouring of water upon his head. [See Northcote and Brownlow's "Roma Sotterranea," Part II., Plate XV.] The passage before us apparently recommends just this mode of performing the rite. If this should be impracticable, then fresh cold water might be similarly used [in a font]. If cold water could not be had, warm water would answer. If neither cold nor warm water in sufficient quantity (ankle-deep) could be had, then pouring only (the feet resting on the floor or ground) would suffice. This last is now the Syrian mode of baptism, and probably always has been. This fact, ascertained by the Crusaders (in the third Crusade, 1189–92), and made known through them in Europe, would help to account for Aquinas's definition of baptism, so different from that of Peter Lombard

NOTES.

about a century before. Lombard's definition requires immersion ; Aquinas's definition permits either immersion, pouring, or sprinkling. The Seventh Book of the Apostolic Constitutions, at this point (Section xxii.), says nothing about the mode, but prescribes anointing with oil, both before and after baptism. Fasting is enjoined in both documents.

CHAP. VIII.

P. 14, l. 154.—παρασκευήν] Cf. John xix. 14.

Wednesday and Friday are named as days of fasting, instead of Monday and Thursday, as observed by "the hypocrites." The Lord's Prayer ends with the Doxology, as in Matthew, instead of its being omitted, as in Luke.

CHAPS. IX., X.

These two chapters contain a brief eucharistic liturgy.

CHAP. XI.

Apostles and Prophets are described as mere evangelists, or itinerant preachers, who were not expected to remain in one place more than a single day.

P. 20, l. 218.—εἰ μή has been inserted in the translation before ἡμέραν. So Harnack, *Theol. Lit. Zeit.*, Feb. 9, 1884. Cf. p. 22, l. 246.

CHAP. XII.

P. 22, l. 244.—"Ye shall have understanding right and left"] That is, a complete understanding. See 2 Cor. vi. 7.

CHAP. XIII.

Prophets and teachers are here spoken of as resident ministers, entitled to maintenance. They were to have the first-fruits of everything. Σιτία, in Classic Greek, is the plural of σιτίον, meaning "food" in general. Here, as in the Byzantine Greek, it is a singular noun, and means "batch," or "baking of bread."

CHAP. XIV.

The Lord's Day is the day for worship and for the Eucharist. No mention is made of the seventh day of the week.

CHAP. XV.

P. 26, l. 277.—"Now appoint for yourselves," χειροτονήσατε οὖν ἑαυτοῖς] Χειροτονέω occurs only twice in the New Testament (Acts xiv. 23 ; 2 Cor. viii. 19), and, in both places, means simply to "appoint." Josephus uses the word in the same sense in Ant. xiii. 2, 2, where Alexander Balas, the pretended son of Antiochus Epiphanes, "appoints" Jonathan High Priest. The same meaning appears in Ant. vii. 9, 3 ; vii. 11, 1. In Ant. vi. 5, 4, however, the noun χειροτονία is used of the coronation of Saul. In Josephus, accordingly, the *prevailing* sense of χειροτονέω is to "appoint." This is the meaning of the word also in the Epistles of Ignatius (about 115 A.D.). See Philadelphians, Chap. 10 ; Smyrnæans, Chap. 11 ; Polycarp, Chap. 7.

But in the "Apostolic Canons," I. and II., and in the "Apostolic Constitutions," viii. 4, 5, χειροτονέω means to "ordain." This represents the usage of the third century, as the New Testament, Josephus, and Ignatius represent the usage of the first and second centuries.

Now, it is noteworthy, that in the "Apostolic Constitutions," vii. 31 (the section corresponding to the passage before us), the word employed is not χειροτονέω, which then meant "ordain," but προχειρίζομαι, a new usage having obtained. In this fifteenth chapter of the "Teaching," χειροτονέω is employed, evidently, in its original sense of "appoint." This indicates the high antiquity of the document, antedating by decades, if not by a whole century, the "Apostolic Canons" and the "Apostolic Constitutions."

As for the officers to be "appointed," only Bishops and Deacons are mentioned. By Bishops must, of course, be meant Presbyters, or Elders. There is no sign of a Bishop as distinguished from a Presbyter; nor of a Ruling Elder as distinguished from a Teaching Elder; and, apparently, there was in each congregation a plurality both of Bishops (or Elders) and Deacons.

CHAP. XVI.

The document concludes with a vision of the Lord coming upon the clouds of heaven, and all the saints with him. The resurrection is of the dead, νεκρῶν, though "not of all the dead." Not a word is said of any second resurrection. If there is to be a second resurrection, it is only implied. Of course, no interval is indicated. Premillennarianism, accordingly, is not directly, perhaps not even indirectly, taught. Following the lead of the New Testament, as in Matt. xxiv. 31, and in 1 Thess. iv. 13–18, our document may, after all, only be emphasizing the resurrection of the righteous.

ERRORS IN THE CODEX CORRECTED BY BRYENNIOS.

	CODEX.	BRYENNIOS.
LINE.		
32.	δέ	δή.
32.	ἱδρωτάτω	ἱδρωσάτω.
51.	ὀργῖλος	ὀργίλος.
59.	εἰδωλολατρίαν	εἰδωλολατρείαν.
62.	εἰδωλολατρία	εἰδωλολατρεία.
91.	ἡ	δ.
103.	δοῦλοι [Sic! See Bryenn., p. 22, N. 19]	δοῦλοι.
104.	ἡμῶν	ὑμῶν.
114, 115.	εἰδωλολατρίαι	εἰδωλολατρεῖαι.
115.	φαρμακίαι [1]	φαρμακεῖαι.
158, 159.	γεννηθήτω	γενηθήτω.
188.	ὑμῶν	ἡμῶν.
197.	σὺ ἡ δόξα	σοὶ ἡ δόξα.
205.	ὡς ἀννὰ τῷ θεῷ	ὡσαννὰ τῷ υἱῷ.
229.	ὁ ῥίζων	ὀρίζων.
244.	ἔξεται	ἔξετε.
258.	δώσεις τὴν ἀπαρχήν	δώσεις.

[1] Used only in poetry.—*Bryenn.*

37